Terry O'Brien

Bridge to College English

文法中心の大学英語

by

Kei Mihara / Yukiko Fukumoto / Hidenori Muramatsu / Hiroshi Kimura

NAN'UN-DO

Bridge to College English

by

Terry O'Brien

Kei Mihara / Yukiko Fukumoto / Hidenori Muramatsu / Hiroshi Kimura

© 2003　All Rights Reserved

はしがき

　ロンドンや田舎の街並みを彩る癒しの風景は、イギリスを訪れる人たちを快く迎えてくれます。時は過ぎても、ロンドンの街並みは昔のままだし、田園風景はどこまでも美しいままです。かつて、イギリスの詩人、キーツは「明るく開けた空を見るのは、なんと甘く気持ちのいいことか」と言いましたが、イギリスを旅し、のどかな風景に浮かぶ空を見上げると、不思議に、ふとそんな気持ちになります。

　本書で、イギリスの旅をしながら、いま一度、やさしい文法のポイントをチェックしてみましょう。なかなか越えられない英語学習の壁。その壁を打ち破ってくれるのが、まず、しっかりと身につけた文法力とリスニング力です。肩の力をぬき、リラックスして、英語コミュニケーション能力を確実にアップしましょう。

○本書の使い方○

本書は、文法を中心に、やさしい英語で書かれたイギリス情報や各種文法とリスニング練習を通じて、総合的な英語コミュニケーション能力を養うことを目的としています。また、TOEICテスト対策も視野に入れて構成しています。

Warm Up!　写真を見て、質問に対する正しい答えを、CDを聞いて選んでください。
Check!　これだけは知って欲しい、基本的な文法のポイントです。

I Choose or Correct

　文法、語法の理解度をチェックします。1〜5（語彙・文法問題）は空所に入れるのに最も適当な語句を1つ選んでください。また、6〜7（誤文訂正問題）は間違いを含むものを1つ選んでください。

II Read and Answer

　文法のポイントを含む70語程度のやさしい英文を読んでください。また、その内容理解をQ&Aで確認します。質問に対する正しい答えを選んでください。

III Write and Listen

　[A] Arrange the words　文法のポイントを含む会話文の(　)内の語句を正しく並べかえてください。文頭に来る語も小文字にしています。
　[B] Q&A　[A]の会話の内容について、まず、質問をCDで聞き空所に単語を書いてください。そして、質問に対する正しい答えを選んでください。

Do you know?

　文中の(1)〜(3)を英語で書いてください。

　本書により、英語を学ぶ楽しさを肌で感じて英語の海に身をゆだね、さらに、イギリス人とその風景に対する幅広い知識を身につけ、21世紀を生きる若者の視野が広がれば、これに勝る喜びはありません。

2002年　夏　　　　　　　　　　　　　　　　　　　　　　　　　　　　　　　　編著者

Contents

1	**Airport Announcement** 空港では忘れ物にご用心	1 <冠 詞>
2	**A Party** いくつになっても楽しい誕生日	4 <名 詞・代名詞>
3	**Tourists** 疲れても見たいステキな城	7 <It の用法>
4	**A Wedding** 結婚は人生の至福	10 <形容詞>
5	**On Campus** イギリスの夏は日本人がいっぱい	13 <副 詞>
6	**Food** イギリス人と日本人、どちらがよく食べるの？	16 <比 較>
7	**Renting a Car** 車が故障したときはレンタカーで	19 <疑問文>
8	**Asking Directions** 道案内は正確に	22 <命令文>
9	**Liverpool** 聞き取りにくいリバプールのことば	25 <関係代名詞>
10	**Going to a University** 大学生ブライアンの心配ごと	28 <現在時制>
11	**Rain** 雨がよく降るイギリス	31 <過去時制>
12	**Making Plans** 楽しみなロンドンでの休暇	34 <未来時制>
13	**What Are You Doing?** イギリス人はサッカー好き	37 <進行形>
14	**Using a Credit Card** サイフを忘れたら支払いはカードで	40 <完了時制>

15	**Museums** ミュージアムはじっくり見よう	**43** <助動詞>
16	**The News** ちょっと表現が大げさなテレビニュース	**46** <受動態>
17	**In the Park** 休日は広々とした公園で	**49** <to 不定詞>
18	**Walking** 散歩は暖かい格好で行こう	**52** <動名詞>
19	**At a Hairdresser's** 男でも髪をのばしたい	**55** <使役動詞>
20	**Restaurants** レストランで注文を決めるのに、ひと苦労	**58** <some と any>
21	**Hotels** 古くても人気のあるホテル	**61** <接続詞>
22	**Telephones** 故障が多い公衆電話	**64** <前置詞>
23	**Haddon Hall** ダービーシャーにある古くて値打ちのある建物	**67** <数 詞>
24	**Requests** 他人への依頼は丁寧に	**70** <丁寧表現>
25	**Going Home** 帰るときは、みやげものでいっぱい	**73** <付加疑問>

Lesson 1　　　　　　　Airport Announcement

冠　詞
空港では忘れ物にご用心

Warm Up!

1. What is each girl holding in her hand?　　　(A)　　(B)
2. Each suitcase has … ?　　　　　　　　　　(A)　　(B)
3. The tour agent is saying, "Do not lose …. "　(A)　　(B)

 Check!

不定冠詞 a, an と定冠詞 the

1. 不定冠詞は初出の普通名詞、定冠詞は既出の名詞

   Paul bought *a* radio and *a* Walkman, but he gave *the* Walkman to his brother.

2. 無冠詞になるのは、数えられない名詞、複数名詞

   Time is *money*. / I like *oranges*, but my brother prefers *apples*.

3. その他

   70 miles *an* hour （〜につき）

   He took me by *the* hand in the dark. （体の一部）

I Choose or Correct

1. Language is ____ of communication.
   (A) mean   (B) a mean   (C) a means   (D) the means
2. I am ____ majoring in economics.
   (A) freshman   (B) a freshman   (C) freshman's   (D) the freshman
3. Since my house is located near the sea, I go out to ____ almost every day.
   (A) beach   (B) a beach   (C) beach's   (D) the beach
4. I bought _____ yesterday.
   (A) a furniture   (B) many furnitures
   (C) none furniture   (D) some furniture
5. When someone grabbed me _____, I was scared.
   (A) at my arm   (B) by the arm   (C) of arm   (D) with an arm
6. In <u>the past</u> I wanted to be <u>a lifeguard</u>, but now I'm studying to become
       A   B
   <u>the doctor</u>.
       C
7. <u>The development</u> of big cities is causing <u>the serious problems</u> for
           A   B
   <u>future generations</u>.
           C

II Read and Answer

Ladies and gentlemen ... your attention, please! A brown suitcase has been found in the main lobby of the airport. Would the owner of the suitcase please go immediately to the airport enquiries desk on the first floor, or contact an airport staff member? May I remind all passengers that bags must not be left unattended and that passengers must take their bags with them at all times. Thank you.

Q & A

1. What has been found in the airport building?
   (A) A brown bag.   (B) A brown suitcase.
2. Where is the airport enquiries desk?
   (A) On the first floor.   (B) In the main lobby.

III Write and Listen  3

[A] Arrange the words

man: Where are you going to stay?

woman: The hotel is called the Holiday Inn, and ¹(centre, of, in, is, it, London, the), but I don't know the address and phone number.

man: Why ²(a, don't, from, pamphlet, pick, up, you) the information desk over there? ³(address, be, in, it, should, the).

woman: That's a good idea. Thank you.

[B] Q&A

1. What is the (   ) (   ) the hotel?
   (A) The Holiday Inn.   (B) The Holiday Hotel.

2. What doesn't the (   ) (   )?
   (A) Her address.   (B) The address of the hotel.

3. Where can she (   ) (   ) address?
   (A) In a pamphlet.   (B) In the pamphlet.

Do you know?

日本からの下線部⁽¹⁾のほとんどが到着するのが、London の南西郊外にある Heathrow Airport。空港から London の中心部へ最も速く行けるのが、1998年に開通した特急列車⁽²⁾Heathrow Express で、London の Paddington 駅まで約15分。ほかにも地下鉄⁽³⁾やバスを利用できます。

左の文中の下線部を英語にしなさい。

(1) _____

(2) _____

(3) _____

Lesson 2
名詞・代名詞

A Party
いくつになっても楽しい誕生日

Warm Up!

  4

1. How many people are there in the picture?　　(A)　　(B)
2. How many of them are wearing glasses?　　(A)　　(B)
3. Who is shouting to us?　　(A)　　(B)

 Check!

名詞 / 代名詞

1. 数えられる名詞：普通名詞と集合名詞
   I subscribe to two **newspapers**. / **The police** are searching his house.

2. 数えられない名詞：物質名詞、抽象名詞、固有名詞
   We need some **furniture**. / **Beauty** is only skin-deep.

3. 代名詞：人称代名詞 (I, you, he)、指示代名詞 (this, that)、
   不定代名詞 (one, another)
   I lost **my** keys somewhere. Didn't **you** see **them**?
   These are the keys I'm looking for.

I Choose or Correct

1. As I had my bicycle stolen, I bought a new _____ .
   (A) another　　(B) it　　(C) one　　(D) other
2. Even the strongest pesticide has little or no _____ on this kind of insect.
   (A) effect　　(B) effete　　(C) effort　　(D) effuse
3. We need _____ maintenance to keep our air-conditioner running well.
   (A) many　　(B) most　　(C) regular　　(D) singular
4. I know this floppy disk belongs to Emily, but I don't know _____ content.
   (A) her　　(B) its　　(C) it's　　(D) their
5. Despite some _____, this tax reform bill was passed yesterday.
   (A) obedience　　(B) object　　(C) objections　　(D) objectives
6. How <u>much</u> police officers are <u>needed</u> <u>to look after</u> the opening ceremony?
        A   B   C
7. Robert has <u>three</u> cars, but <u>those of them</u> are mainly used by <u>his son</u>.
              A   B   C

II Read and Answer   5

Peter's 50th birthday party was one of the best I have ever been to. We had it in a restaurant. It was a small place but the atmosphere was good. Jennie and Lucy helped with the preparations, and I got there a bit early to help them. The party started at seven, but nobody could remember when it finished. All the guests started by drinking a toast, and then they continued drinking until most of them had too much.

Q & A

1. What kind of place did they have the party in?
   (A) The best restaurant ever.
   (B) A small restaurant with a good atmosphere.
2. What condition were most of the people in at the end of the party?
   (A) They were drunk.　　(B) They felt fine.

III Write and Listen 6

[A] Arrange the words

man: I went to Peter's party last week and it was fantastic.

woman: ¹(else, there, went, who)?

man: His family and a few friends. ²(a, couple, had, I, met, of, only, them) before, but we soon got on well. Boy, we ate too much, and drank too much. Peter was telling jokes, and everybody was laughing at them.

woman: It sounds like you had a great time. Did you give Peter a present?

man: Yes, ³(a, box, gave, him, huge, we), but inside there was a wrist watch. He put it on, so I think he was pleased with it.

[B] Q&A

1. How did the man (   ) (   ) Peter's party?
   (A) They were fantastic.   (B) It was great.

2. What was everybody (   ) (   ) ?
   (A) Peter's guests.   (B) Peter's jokes.

3. What was Peter's (   ) (   ) his present?
   (A) He was pleased.   (B) He was surprised.

Do you know?

ballと呼ばれるフォーマルなパーティー⁽¹⁾は大学でもよく行われます。フルコースの食事⁽²⁾のあとは葉巻まで出され、その後ダンスまたはディスコパーティーが深夜遅くまで続きます。たいていカップルで参加しますが、パーティーの前には、男性がパートナー⁽³⁾の女性に花を贈ります。

(1) _____

(2) _____

(3) _____

Lesson 3

Itの用法

Tourists

疲れても見たいステキな城

Warm Up!

1. Where are the couple? (A) (B)
2. What is the woman looking at? (A) (B)
3. What is all around the couple? (A) (B)

 Check!

非人称のit

1. 時、天候、気温、距離などの状況

   It is Sunday today. / *It*'s very humid. / *It* is ten minutes' walk to the station.

2. 形式主語[目的語]：後続の動名詞、不定詞(句)、名詞句[節]の内容を受ける。

   It is no use cry*ing*. / I found *it* difficult *to* be president. / *It* is clear *that* we will win.

3. 成句：it is ... that (強調構文)、call it a day「終わりにする」、walk it「徒歩で行く」

   It is James that wrote the report. / *It*'s six o'clock, so let's call *it* a day.

I Choose or Correct

1. It is standard business practice _____ the day's schedule every morning.
   (A) check   (B) for checking   (C) that check   (D) to check
2. Jeremy found _____ difficult to write down foreign names.
   (A) him   (B) himself   (C) it   (D) them
3. I'd appreciate _____ if you could give me written permission to use your room.
   (A) not   (B) it   (C) that   (D) very
4. _____ without saying that we cannot live without water.
   (A) It went   (B) It goes   (C) They go   (D) They'll go
5. My mother scolded me, but it was my sister _____ was to blame.
   (A) for   (B) to   (C) which   (D) who
6. The warmer <u>it becomes</u>, the less <u>it will cost</u> us <u>of heat</u> our house.
        A   B   C
7. <u>It'll take</u> more than two hours <u>of get to</u> our office <u>if</u> there is heavy traffic
        A   B   C
   on the road.

II Read and Answer   8

It is difficult for tourists to come to this castle because there are no trains or buses around here. But it is surprising how many people visit this place every year. It takes at least a couple of hours to walk around the castle, and it is worth spending a long time looking at the gardens. George and his wife came here by car this morning, and they are standing on the bridge in the sunshine.

Q & A

1. Why is this tourist spot so difficult to get to?
   (A) There are not many buses.   (B) Because there are no trains or buses.
2. How long does it take to look around the castle?
   (A) More than a couple of hours.   (B) Within two hours.

III Write and Listen

[A] Arrange the words

wife: George, it was beautiful. I know ¹(a, it, long, around, to, time, took, walk) the castle, but I think it was worth it. Don't you?

husband: Oh, yes, absolutely, and it was cheap too.

wife: We were lucky ²(a, because, day, such, it, warm and lovely, was). It was perfect.

husband: Look, it's getting late and I'm hungry. How ³(a, about, eat, for, looking, lunch, place, to)?

wife: My goodness, it's after three. Let's go.

[B] Q&A

1. What was the (   ) (   ) during their visit?
   (A) It was a great day.　　　(B) It was too hot.

2. How did George (   ) (   ) the castle?
   (A) It was beautiful and cheap.　　(B) It was beautiful but expensive.

3. What are they going to (   ) (   ) now?
   (A) Go to eat lunch.　　(B) Continue to look at the castle.

Do you know?

イギリスにはあちこちに⁽¹⁾お城がありますが、最も有名なのは 900年もの間イングランド王の城としてそびえる Windsor Castle でしょう。また "The loveliest castle in the world" ともいわれる Leeds Castle は、なだらかな⁽²⁾緑の丘と湖のほとりで小さくて優雅な⁽³⁾たたずまいを見せています

(1)

(2) _____

(3)

Lesson 4　　　　　　　　A Wedding

形容詞　　　　　　　　結婚は人生の至福

Warm  　　　　　　　　　　　　　　 10

1. What does the sign on the rear of the car say?　　(A)　(B)
2. What is unusual about this car?　　(A)　(B)
3. What do you think these two people have just done?　　(A)　(B)

形容詞

1. 限定用法と叙述用法：名詞を限定したり、動詞の補語として用いられる。
   This is a *beautiful* lake. ／ This lake is *beautiful*.

2. 一方の用法しかないもの： elder, only, main は限定用法
   　　　　　　　　　　　　asleep, alive, alike は叙述用法
   This is the *main* road. ／ His old dog is still *alive*.

3. 語順：数量＋大小＋形状＋性質＋新旧(年齢)＋色＋材料
   three small pretty white cups ／ *five high old wooden* buildings

I Choose or Correct

1. We should carry out a ____ investigation of the security system every year.
   (A) though (B) thorough (C) thoroughly (D) through
2. Due to the long spell of dry weather, they are suffering from a ____ shortage of water.
   (A) server (B) seven (C) sever (D) severe
3. I'm going to wear a ____ tie tomorrow.
   (A) green silk new (B) new green silk
   (C) silk new green (D) silk green new
4. Albert and William are very much ____. I can't tell them apart.
   (A) alibi (B) alien (C) alike (D) alive
5. Yesterday, dozens of ____ young people were dancing here.
   (A) livable (B) livelong (C) lively (D) livery
6. While <u>traveling around</u> Europe, I found out <u>my English</u> was not <u>enough good</u>.
       A   B   C
7. Tom <u>is absent</u> <u>without notice</u>. I wonder if <u>something seriously</u>
         A   B   C
   happened to him.

II Read and Answer

 11

Paul and Sally have just got married. They are sitting in a white, open-top, vintage Bentley. The ceremony was at a beautiful old church in the attractive village of Underwood. Sally is wearing a long, white, low-cut wedding dress, and has a diamond tiara and a single strand, pearl necklace. Her father is the owner of a large and successful printing company, and he has given the newlyweds a new house with a small swimming pool in the garden.

Q & A

1. What was Sally wearing?
   (A) A long, white, wedding dress. (B) A low-cut diamond tiara.
2. What did her father give them for a wedding present?
   (A) A large house with a small garden.
   (B) A house with a small swimming pool.

III Write and Listen

[A] Arrange the words

man: They had a lovely wedding, and I think Paul is a very lucky man.

woman: Yes, I agree. Her father is rich. That's why ¹(a, gave, he, house, nice, such, them).

man: Did you know it is Paul's second marriage?

woman: Good heavens. No, I didn't. That comes as quite a big surprise. So, ²(doing, first, his, is, now, what, wife)?

man: She is very happy too, because ³(a, also, family, into, married, she, well-to-do) last month.

[B] Q&A

1. Why do (　　　　) (　　　　) Paul is a very lucky man?

    (A) Sally's father is a wealthy man.　(B) The wedding was lovely.

2. (　　　　) (　　　　) times had Paul been married before?

    (A) Once.　(B) Twice.

3. Why is Paul's (　　　　) (　　　　) happy?

    (A) Because she got married.　(B) She married into money.

Do you know?

イギリスの結婚式は大きく分けて二通り⁽¹⁾、教会での式と役所 (registry office) での宗教色のない式とがあります。結婚証明書⁽²⁾は結婚式を行わない限り発行されないので、簡単にregistry officeですませる人も増えています。さまざまな結婚式やパーティの様子は、映画⁽³⁾ "Four Weddings and a Funeral" (「フォーウエディング」1994) で楽しめます。

(1) _____

(2) _____

(3) _____

Lesson 5　　　　　　　　　On Campus

副　詞

イギリスの夏は日本人がいっぱい

Warm 　　　　　　　　　　　　 13

1. What do most of them have on their backs?　　(A)　　(B)
2. What is the weather like?　　　　　　　　　　(A)　　(B)
3. Where are the people walking?　　　　　　　　(A)　　(B)

 Check!

副　詞

1. 動詞、形容詞、他の副詞を修飾：通例、形容詞+ly の形を取る。
   Speak *slowly* and *clearly*. / *Luckily* I got the first prize.

2. 要注意の副詞：hard (熱心に) と hardly (ほとんど〜ない)、near (近く) と nearly (あやうく)
   John worked *hard* to get a promotion. / John *hardly* studied when he was young.

3. 修飾の違い：very は形容詞・副詞と現在分詞 (〜ing)、much は比較級と過去分詞 (-ed)
   I'm *very* happy. / I'm *much* happier than before.

I Choose or Correct

1. Nancy is usually very punctual, but this morning she got up _____.
    (A) late   (B) lately   (C) latest   (D) more late
2. Paul is _____ punctual. Sometimes he makes me wait more than 30 minutes!
    (A) always   (B) ever   (C) near   (D) not always
3. I think Bob's theory is not only original but _____ interesting too.
    (A) high   (B) highly   (C) many   (D) much
4. Believe me, this is the _____ best thing I can do now.
    (A) many   (B) most   (C) much   (D) very
5. Mt. Fuji is a very high mountain, but Mt. Chomolungma is _____ higher.
    (A) many   (B) most   (C) much   (D) very
6. I think I've met her <u>ago</u>, but I can't remember <u>clearly</u> <u>when and where</u>.
           A   B   C
7. While I was driving <u>home</u>, I <u>near</u> hit a deer that <u>suddenly</u> appeared on
                        A   B   C
the road.

II Read and Answer   14

Kenji is spending the summer at an English university. He often hangs around with his Japanese friends, and hardly ever speaks English outside class. He thinks his lessons are hard. His teacher, Patty, is really very kind, but Kenji almost never understands her. Yesterday, he completely forgot about his homework, so Patty will probably speak to him angrily in the next class.

Q & A

1. How often does Kenji speak English outside his classes?
    (A) Sometimes.   (B) Almost never.
2. How does Kenji feel about his lessons?
    (A) He thinks they are difficult.
    (B) He thinks his lessons are lots of fun.

III Write and Listen

[A] Arrange the words

Alan: Hi there, Kenji. ¹(class, going, how, is, your)?

Kenji: Not very well, I'm afraid. ²(better, English, everybody, me, much, speaks, than).

Alan: How often do you prepare for your lessons... you know, like, reading through your textbooks?

Kenji: Hm ... ³(course, couple of, days, first, for, I, of, that, the, the, tried), but recently, never.

Alan: Well, obviously you are having problems. You should definitely talk to your teacher about it.

[B] Q&A

1. How is Kenji's English (   ) (   ) his classmates?
   (A) Kenji speaks better.   (B) Kenji speaks worse than they do.

2. (   ) (   ) does Kenji read his textbooks before class?
   (A) Every day.   (B) He used to but he stopped.

3. (   ) (   ) did Alan give him?
   (A) Consult your teacher.   (B) Take a couple of days off.

Do you know?

イギリスの大学では夏に多彩な⁽¹⁾summer schoolが開かれています。語学はもちろん、文学、歴史、美術、音楽、スポーツ、山歩きに至るまで、国籍⁽²⁾・年齢を問わず参加することができ、期間もさまざまです。いつか留学してみたいと思えば、旅行を兼ねて行きたい大学のサマーコース⁽³⁾に参加してみるのもいいでしょう。

(1) _____

(2) _____

(3) _____

Lesson 6　　　　　　　　　Food

比較
イギリス人と日本人、どちらがよく食べるの？

1. How many paper cups are there on this table?　　(A)　(B)
2. The girl on the left is wearing ....　　　　　　　　(A)　(B)
3. The girl in the middle ....　　　　　　　　　　　　(A)　(B)

比較構文

1. 同等比較：as +形容詞[副詞]+ as で、程度が同じであることを表す。
    George is *as* tall *as* his father. / Ken speaks English *as* fluently *as* Americans.

2. 比較級：比較級+thanで、程度に差があることを表す。
    強調には、even, far, much を使う。
    Bob's bag is much ***heavier than*** mine. / I usually get up ***earlier than*** my brother.

3. 最上級：the[one's]+形容詞の最上級、副詞の最上級で、1番であることを表す。
    強調はby far
    Bill is ***our youngest*** child. / Linda runs ***fastest***. / Mariah is ***by far the most popular***.

I Choose or Correct

1. The population of London is _____ that of Birmingham.
   (A) large as   (B) as larger   (C) larger than   (D) more large than
2. Diana is _____ runner in her class, but her brother runs much faster.
   (A) faster   (B) fastest   (C) the fastest   (D) the most fast
3. All the applicants are well qualified, but Mr. Brown is by far _____ candidate.
   (A) better   (B) best   (C) the best   (D) the most
4. I made enough money at the previous company, but now I make twice _____ .
   (A) as many   (B) as much   (C) much more   (D) more than
5. I would appreciate receiving the details as soon _____ .
   (A) as can   (B) as I will   (C) as possible   (D) as probable
6. Don's presentation was <u>superior than</u> <u>his coworkers</u>', though he was
                          A   B
   <u>the youngest</u>.
         C
7. Today's air-conditioners require <u>much less</u> electricity <u>as</u> <u>those twenty</u>
                                        A   B
   <u>years ago</u>.
         C

II Read and Answer   17

Which is better, eating in England or Japan? In restaurants in England there are fewer items on the menu, there is more food on your plate, and the desserts are much sweeter too. Although Japanese people eat more rice than the English, the Japanese consume much less food. Meals in the UK are cheaper than in Japan. Is that why English people eat more food than the Japanese?

Q & A

1. People in England eat ... the Japanese.
   (A) less rice than   (B) more rice than
2. Eating in Japan is ... in England.
   (A) a little cheaper than   (B) more expensive than

III Write and Listen 18

[A] Arrange the words

Anne: How come you always have more than me? You eat faster than me, and then you steal from my plate.

Yumi: Oh I am sorry, but I just love these french fries. I can't stop eating them. They ¹(are, best, ever, had, I've, the). You don't mind, do you?

Anne: No, not really, but you ²(are, each, eating and drinking, day, more, much, than) me.

Yumi: Yes, I suppose you are right. I'm getting fatter and fatter recently. I really ³(a, bit, lose, of, should, weight). Um ... I wonder how I can do that?

Anne: That's easy. Spend less and eat less. And don't eat my french fries!

[B] Q&A

1. Yumi (　　　) (　　　) ....

    (A) and more than Anne　　(B) but only as much as Anne

2. What is Yumi's (　　　) (　　　) recently?

    (A) She is spending too much money.　(B) She is putting on weight.

3. Yumi should (　　　) (　　　) ....

    (A) her food expenses　　(B) only french fries

Do you know?

イギリスでは小さな売店⁽¹⁾でも買えるくらいおなじみなのに、イギリス料理としてあまり知られていないのが Cornish Pasties。肉、野菜、香辛料⁽²⁾が入ったパイで、もともとコーンウォール地方の鉱夫や農夫の持ち運びに便利なお弁当でした。右半分に肉と野菜、左半分にフルーツをつめたメインとデザート⁽³⁾が合体したものもあります。

(1) _____

(2) _____

(3) _____

Lesson 7　　　　　　　　　Renting a car

疑問文
車が故障したときはレンタカーで

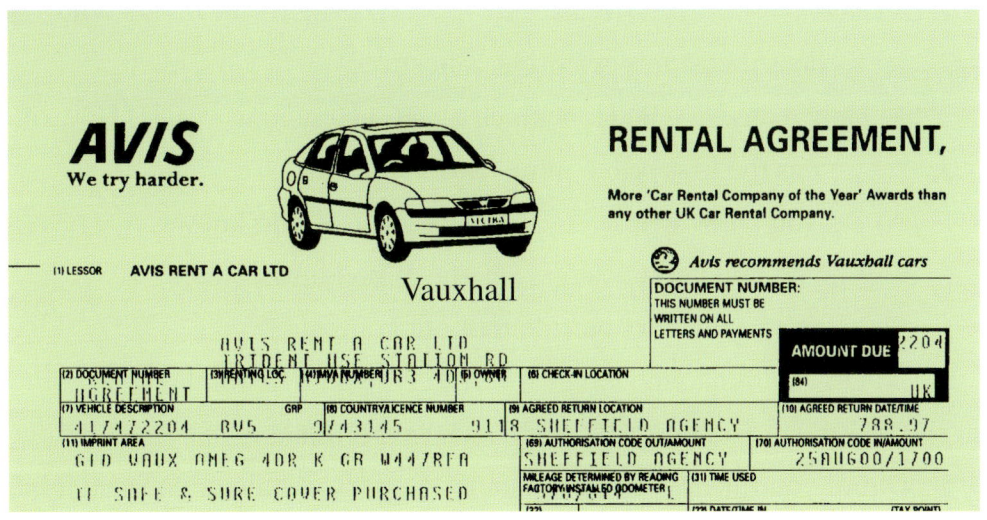

Warm Up!

 19

1. What is the name of this car rental company?　　　(A)　(B)
2. What kind of car does the company rent out?　　　(A)　(B)
3. What must you fill out and sign before you rent a car?　(A)　(B)

 Check!

疑問文

1. Yes/No 疑問文：Do you ...? などの形を取り、yes か no で答える。
   Do you smoke? / ***Can you*** finish this report by Friday?

2. 疑問詞を用いた疑問文：what, which, who, when, where, why, how で始まる。
   Which do you recommend? / ***How*** can I get to the station?

3. 否定疑問文：Didn't you ...? などの形を取る。答え方に注意が必要
   Haven't you filled out this form? ─ Yes, I have.(記入した) / No, I haven't.(してない)

I Choose or Correct

1. _____ do you prefer, e-mail or fax?
   (A) How (B) What (C) Which (D) Who
2. _____ does it cost to get a driver's licence?
   (A) How many (B) How much (C) How long (D) How often
3. _____ was the first prime minister of the U.K.?
   (A) Do you know who (B) Do you who knows
   (C) Who do you know (D) Who knows
4. _____ will be the next president of our company?
   (A) Do you think who (B) Do you who think
   (C) Who do you think (D) Who thinks
5. "Didn't you finish your term paper?" "_____ . I already turned it in."
   (A) I'm afraid not (B) I'm afraid so
   (C) Of course not (D) Yes, of course
6. "<u>How</u> hasn't the plane <u>arrived</u>?" "Because there is a strong wind <u>blowing</u>."
       A   B   C
7. <u>Do you think</u> <u>how many</u> branch offices <u>your company has</u>?
        A   B   C

II Read and Answer 20

> Mr. Barnsley wants to rent a car for two weeks because his car has broken down. He is a businessman and every day he travels around different cities visiting his customers, so he must have a car. "Now then, which car hire company is near here? I think I'll check in the Yellow Pages .... Ah, here is one. I'll give them a call right now," he is saying to himself.

Q & A

1. Why does Mr. Barnsley need a car?
   (A) He has to drive each day. (B) He is a visitor in this city.
2. What is he trying to find in the Yellow Pages?
   (A) A car hire company. (B) A garage to repair his car.

III Write and Listen

[A] Arrange the words

A: Hello. You are Mr. Barnsley?

B: Yes, that's right ... Alfred Barnsley. I ¹(a, about, car, earlier, renting, phoned).

A: How long do you want one for, and ²(do, kind, of, vehicle, want, what, you)?

B: Er ... something like a 1500, four door and automatic ... if you've got one. Oh, and I want it for two weeks.

A: Well, we've got a nice clean Vauxhall available, but it's an 1800. Is that all right? It's the red one over there at the end.

B: Yes, that's fine. I'll take that one. Now, ³(be, how, including, insurance, it, much, the, will)?

[B] Q&A

1. When did Mr. Barnsley (   ) (   ) car hire company?
   (A) A week ago.   (B) A short time ago.

2. (   ) (   ) of car is he going to hire?
   (A) A red 1500.   (B) An 1800 Vauxhall.

3. How long does he want (   ) (   ) the car for?
   (A) Two weeks.   (B) Just for the day.

Do you know?

イギリスの交通規則⁽¹⁾は日本とほぼ同じですが、注意が必要なのが roundabout。日本でいうロータリーですが、交差点⁽²⁾のかわりにあちこちにあります。進入するときは必ず左折し⁽³⁾、右からの車が優先。中に入ってしまえば、行く方向が定まるまで何度でもぐるぐる回ればよいのです。慣れれば、とても効率の良いしくみだと感心します。

(1) _____

(2) _____

(3) _____

Lesson 8　　　　　　　　Asking Directions

命令文
道案内は正確に

Warm  　　　　　　　　　　　　　　　　　　 22

1. Where are the universities?　　　　　　　　　　　(A)　(B)
2. If you want to get on a bus, you should ....　　　　(A)　(B)
3. Where is the nearest telephone box?　　　　　　　(A)　(B)

 **Check!**

命令文

1. 直接命令：主語を用いず、原形動詞か Don't～、Never～で始める。
   Get away at once. / ***Don't be*** so irritated. / ***Never give up***.

2. Youを表示：いらだちや怒りを表す失礼な表現
   You come here. / ***You tell*** me why.

3. 間接命令：must, should, had better などを用い、間接的に命令を表す。
   You ***must*** come back by 10 o'clock. / You***'d better*** apologize.

I Choose or Correct

1. ____ quiet, or I'll make you get out of here.
   (A) Be (B) Do (C) Did (D) Not
2. If you take a taxi, ____ sure to get a receipt. We'll reimburse you your fare.
   (A) are (B) be (C) do (D) never
3. I'm sorry, but I'm not in charge of this matter. ____ Mr. Johnson about it.
   (A) Ask (B) Asks (C) Does (D) Does ask
4. When you find out what the problem is, ____ me at once.
   (A) do tell (B) telling (C) tells (D) will tell
5. "I'm sorry, but Liz is out now. Would you like to leave a message?"
   " ____ that I called."
   (A) Did tell her (B) Didn't tell her (C) Just tell her (D) Hardly tell her
6. I think it is nice to say, "Take care and takes it easy," when you say
                              A   B
   good-bye to someone.
   C
7. Margaret, listen to me. Please do sensible. This is not your business,
              A   B
   mind you.
   C

II Read and Answer 23

I'm sorry? You said you want to find the nearest dentist? Well then ... er, go straight down this road until you come to the traffic signals. Turn left, and then take the second right. Keep going along there and at the end of the road turn left, and you'll see the dentist on your left. It's a small building, but there's a big sign outside the door, so you can't miss it.

Q & A

1. Where should the person go after the traffic signals?
   (A) Turn left and take the second right.
   (B) Turn right and take the second left.
2. Why is the dentist's easy to find?
   (A) It is near the traffic lights. (B) There's a big sign outside.

III Write and Listen

[A] Arrange the words

woman: Excuse me, could you ¹(is, post office, tell, the, me, where), please?

man: Sure. It's opposite the library. Cross the ²(and, down, go, here, straight, street) there. Turn right at the bookstore, and the post office is the third or fourth shop on your right.

woman: So, I go right at the bookshop?

man: That's right. You ³(can, from, here, it, see). It's the red building on the corner. Turn right there.

woman: Right. Thanks a lot.

[B] Q&A

1. (   ) (   ) opposite the library?
    (A) A bookstore.　　(B) The post office.
2. (   ) (   ) the woman want to go?
    (A) To the post office.　　(B) To a bookstore.
3. (   ) (   ) times did the two people say "right"?
    (A) Six times.　　(B) Twice.

Do you know?

イギリスではすべての通りに名前がついています。ロンドンには "London A to Z" という地図がどこにでも売っていて、目的地⁽¹⁾を探すのに便利です。また道路にはM(Motorway)のつく高速道路、Aのつく幹線道路⁽²⁾、それ以外のB道路があります。M、A、Bの後に数字がつきます。高速道路は基本的に無料⁽³⁾です。

(1) _____

(2) _____

(3) _____

Lesson 9   Liverpool

関係代名詞

聞き取りにくいリバプールのことば

Warm

 25

1. What are hanging on the walls of this building?　(A)　(B)
2. There are four … above this shop's entrance.　(A)　(B)
3. What does "ST" stand for?　(A)　(B)

 Check!

関係代名詞

1. 人を先行詞とする関係代名詞：who, whose, whom, that
   I met a boy ***who*** said he was your son.
   This is Jim, ***who*** is our guest speaker today.

2. 物を先行詞とする関係代名詞：which, whose, that
   This is a letter ***which*** he left here.
   This is the only newspaper ***that*** covers the news.

3. Which の特殊用法：..., which で、前文の内容を受ける。
   Lynn said she passed the exam, ***which*** turned out to be a lie.

I Choose or Correct

1. I am looking for someone _____ will help me run my company.
   (A) what (B) which (C) who (D) whose
2. Where is the report _____ I asked you to complete this morning?
   (A) which (B) who (C) whom (D) whose
3. This is all the money _____ I have now.
   (A) that (B) what (C) which (D) whose
4. We had eight applicants, none of _____ was well qualified.
   (A) that (B) what (C) which (D) whom
5. Eric, _____ is our accountant, completed this balance sheet.
   (A) that (B) what (C) who (D) whom
6. Albert <u>founded</u> his company in 1971, <u>that</u> his son succeeded <u>to</u> 25 years later.
      A   B   C
7. In <u>this</u> country, <u>this</u> is the only weekly magazine <u>which</u> contains no
      A   B   C
   photographs.

II Read and Answer 26

Liverpool is one of the most famous cities in England. It is the birthplace of the Beatles, whose songs have been popular all over the world since the 1960s. It is the kind of city that not everybody likes. The people who live there speak in a rough dialect that is amusing to listen to yet difficult to understand. Liverpudlians are well known for their sense of humour which has helped them through their hard times.

Q & A

1. What has helped to make Liverpool become a famous city?
   (A) It was the Beatles' hometown.
   (B) There are many songs about Liverpool.
2. What are Liverpudlians famous for?
   (A) Their sense of humour. (B) Their rough dialect.

III Write and Listen 27

[A] Arrange the words

Arthur: Do you know there are a lot of people who live around here that never think twice about making too much noise.

Betty: What do you mean?

Arthur: All day people play music ¹(can, burst, on, stereos, that, your) eardrums. They are the kind of people that I could do without. And the driver of the van ²(always, house, my, outside, parked, that's,) never switches his engine off. I think he is trying to kill me.

Betty: Um ... what you need is ³(a, away, from, good, holiday, this) area.

[B] Q&A

1. Why doesn't Arthur like the people (   ) (   ) near him?

   (A) They always think too much.   (B) They make too much noise.

2. What is the problem that Arthur (   ) (   ) the van driver?

   (A) The driver always keeps his engine running.   (B) The driver is noisy.

3. What is the (   ) (   ) Betty gives to Arthur?

   (A) Switch off your engine.   (B) Take a holiday.

Do you know?

Liverpoolはロンドンの北西300kmに位置するイギリス第2の貿易港⁽¹⁾で、産業革命時代に発展した街です。The Beatles を生んだ街⁽²⁾として有名で、彼らはこの街のクラブ "The Cavern" でデビューしました。最近ではイギリスサッカーの強豪チーム "Liverpool" に所属する⁽³⁾Michael Owenの活躍が注目を集めています。

(1) _____

(2) _____

(3) _____

Lesson 10　　　　　Going to a University

現在時制

大学生ブライアンの心配ごと

Warm Up!

1. What is on the right of this picture?　　　　(A)　(B)
2. What is in front of this university building?　(A)　(B)
3. There are ... cars in front of this bulding.　　(A)　(B)

Check!

現在時制

1. **現在の状態**：be動詞などの状態を表す動詞を現在形で使い、現在の状態を表す。
   This room *is* very hot. / I *have* a cold.

2. **現在の習慣**：動作を表す動詞を現在形で使うと、それが現在の習慣であることを表す。
   John *goes* to college. / I *get up* at seven in the morning.

3. **普遍の真理**：客観的な真理は現在形で表し、時制の一致 (cf. Lesson11) も受けない。
   The earth *is* round. / The sun *rises* in the east.

I Choose or Correct

1. Tracy _____ the sales meeting every Friday.
   (A) attend   (B) attends   (C) is attending   (D) is being attended
2. Paul was quite right when he said one and one _____ two.
   (A) is made   (B) makes   (C) making   (D) will be made
3. I usually walk to my office but _____ a taxi today because I have a cold.
   (A) taken   (B) takes   (C) took   (D) would take
4. I usually eat Chinese food for lunch, but today I _____ French food for a change.
   (A) ate   (B) eaten   (C) eats   (D) would eat
5. Jane and I _____ part time as waitresses at the restaurant.
   (A) has worked   (B) work   (C) working   (D) would work
6. I <u>will stay</u> home if it <u>will rain</u> this afternoon, but I <u>will go hiking</u> anyway tomorrow.
      A   B   C
7. Bill didn't know it <u>was</u> Galileo Galilei who <u>finds</u> that the earth <u>revolves</u> around the sun.
                        A   B   C

II Read and Answer

Brian is a student in this university. He usually arrives half an hour before his lectures and meets his friends in the cafeteria where they drink coffee. After that, they all go to one of the computer rooms and check their mail. Classes begin at nine, but Brian's last classes often finish late, so he doesn't have much time to do his homework at night. That's why he looks worried.

Q & A

1. What do Brian and his friends do first when they meet each other in the mornings?
   (A) They drink coffee in the cafeteria.
   (B) They go straight to their classes.
2. Why does Brian seem to be a little unhappy?
   (A) Because he is late for class.
   (B) Because he doesn't have enough time to do his homework.

III Write and Listen 🎧 30

[A] Arrange the words

teacher: Hello Brian. How are you? Now then, ¹(hand, homework, in, late, often, you, your). That's not good enough. Can you tell me why you do that?

Brian: I'm sorry, but I live on the other side of town, so ²(a, back, get, it, long, me, takes, time, to) home.

teacher: Oh really! When ³(do, get, home, Mondays, on, you)?

Brian: Not until after ten.

teacher: And on Tuesdays?

Brian: At about four.

[B] Q&A

1. Why is the teacher a (　　　　) (　　　　) ? Because Brian ....
   (A) gets home late　　　　(B) hands in his homework late

2. When does Brian (　　　　) (　　　　) home on Mondays?
   (A) After ten.　　　　(B) Before ten.

3. What is (　　　　) (　　　　) ?
   (A) He lives a long way away.　　　　(B) He is very sorry.

Do you know?

イギリスの大学はロンドンを除いて、広々としたキャンパスをもつところが多く、学内に森⁽¹⁾や小さな湖があったりするので、ウサギやリス⁽²⁾が姿を見せるなか、学生は自転車で移動しています。大教室では夜遅くまで⁽³⁾映画や劇が上映されたり、学内の cafe や pub でパーティをしたり、学生の entertainment の場にもなっています。

(1) _____

(2) _____

(3) _____

Lesson 11

過去時制

Rain

雨がよく降るイギリス

Warm Up!

31

1. What were the girls looking at from there?　(A)　(B)
2. What was the weather like?　(A)　(B)
3. What were the people holding in their hands?　(A)　(B)

Check!

過去時制

1. 過去の状態や動作：すでに過去のものとなった状態や動作を表す。
   I *got married* when I *was* twenty-nine.

2. 時制の一致：直接話法を間接話法で表現するとき、従属節は主節と同じ時制になる。
   Edward said, "I have three sons." → Edward said that he *had* three sons.

3. 仮定法過去：現在の事実に反する仮定
   (cf. 過去の事実に反する仮定は、仮定法過去完了)
   I wish I *were* a bird.　(cf. If I *had met* you last year, I would have married you.)

I Choose or Correct

1. The price of rice _____ 20% last year.
   (A) has risen　　(B) raise　　(C) rise　　(D) rose

2. My mother had two children when she _____ my age.
   (A) be　　(B) is　　(C) was　　(D) would be

3. James told me three years ago that he _____ twenty years old.
   (A) be　　(B) was　　(C) were　　(D) will be

4. If I _____ you, I would take that job.
   (A) am　　(B) have been　　(C) were　　(D) would be

5. It's about time you _____ to bed.
   (A) go　　(B) have gone　　(C) went　　(D) would go

6. George <u>asked</u> me yesterday if <u>I will go</u> to the party <u>held</u> this weekend.
   　　　　　　A　　　　　　　　　　　B　　　　　　　　　　C

7. I <u>hate</u> Jane because she <u>speaks</u> to me as if she <u>will be</u> my boss.
   　　A　　　　　　　　　　B　　　　　　　　　　　C

II Read and Answer　32

Last night the girls talked about what to see in London. They got up early and went to the railway station. When they left their hotel this morning it was fine, but it started raining the moment they arrived in London. They put up their umbrellas and walked around the famous sites of London. A car splashed through a puddle and soaked Yuriko. She wasn't pleased about that.

Q & A

1. How did the girls go to London?
   (A) They went by bus.　　(B) They went by train.

2. Why did Yuriko get very wet?
   (A) A car splashed through a puddle.　　(B) She forgot her umbrella.

III Write and Listen

[A] Arrange the words

woman: Excuse me, I left my umbrella on the train. I put it on the overhead luggage rack and ¹(about, all, forgot, got, I, it, when) off.

station staff: I see. Which train was that?

woman: The train from London. It arrived at about five.

station staff: What ²(it, kind, of, umbrella, was)?

woman: A blue and green fold-up one. And it had a shiny red handle.

station staff: You didn't have your name and address on it, by any chance, did you?

woman: Well, ³(come, it, of, think, to), yes I did. It was on the handle, er ... in black ink.

[B] Q&A

1. What was the (   ) (   )?
   (A) She missed her train.   (B) She lost her umbrella.

2. Can (   ) (   ) the umbrella?
   (A) It was shiny green.   (B) It was blue and green and collapsable.

3. What kind (   ) (   ) did it have?
   (A) There was only a name on it.
   (B) It had both a name and an address on it.

Do you know?

イギリスの天気は気まぐれ⁽¹⁾で、曇りや雨の日が多いものの、降ってもすぐ晴れ間がのぞいたりします。雨の量もどしゃ降りになる⁽²⁾ことは少ないので、傘を持っていてもささずに、ぱらぱらした雨⁽³⁾に濡れながら歩いている人たちをよく見かけます。夏も短いため、太陽が出るとすぐ肌を出して芝生に寝そべり、束の間の日光を楽しみます。

(1) _____

(2) _____

(3) _____

Lesson 12 — Making Plans

未来時制

楽しみなロンドンでの休暇

Warm Up! 🦆 (CD 34)

1. What is the weather like in this picture? (A) (B)
2. How can you describe Buckingham Palace? It is …. (A) (B)
3. There are no cars or buses here, but there are many …. (A) (B)

Check!

未来時制

1. **未来の予測**：will, be going to を使い、未来の予測、予定や意志を表す。
   According to the weather forecast, it *will* rain tomorrow. / I *will* pass the exam.

2. **近い未来**：現在進行形の形を取り、まもなく生じる事柄を表す。
   The plane *is arriving*. / This dog *is dying*.

3. **時や条件を表す名詞節の中は未来形、副詞節の中は現在形で、未来のことを表す。**
   Do you know when Bill *will arrive*? / Call me when you *arrive* at Heathrow.

I Choose or Correct

1. Interest rates ____ low for at least another two years.
   (A) remained   (B) remains   (C) will remain   (D) would remain
2. In light of these sales figures, the company ____ up with a big loss.
   (A) end   (B) ended   (C) ending   (D) will end
3. Mr. Turner is out now, and I don't know when he ____ in the office.
   (A) be back   (B) is back   (C) is being back   (D) will be back
4. Would you ask our boss if a meeting ____ tomorrow afternoon?
   (A) be held   (B) being held   (C) will be held   (D) would be held
5. If it ____ this weekend, shall we go skiing together?
   (A) be snowing   (B) snow   (C) snows   (D) will snow
6. When I <u>reached</u> the station, the train <u>left</u>, so I <u>shouted</u>, "Stop!"
          A   B   C
7. James <u>will be</u> five when his next birthday <u>will come</u>, but he thinks
            A   B
   <u>he'll be</u> six.
      C

II Read and Answer CD 35

Peter and Barbara are on holiday in London, and they want to look at the famous sites of the city. Tomorrow morning they are going to get up early and are going to look at Buckingham Palace. After that, they think they will take a walk through St. James's Park and eat lunch on the grass. Peter said, "Do you think the weather will be fine tomorrow? Oh, and shall I set the alarm clock to ring at 6:00?"

Q & A

1. Where do they think they will have lunch?
   (A) On the grass in St. James's Park.   (B) In Buckingham Palace.
2. What does Peter offer to do?
   (A) To set the alarm clock for 6:00.   (B) To wake up feeling fine.

III Write and Listen 🎧 36

[A] Arrange the words

A: Peter, Peter! Wake up! It's already seven o'clock. We are going to be late.

B: Oh, sorry dear. I'll get up right away. Do you think ¹(breakfast, eat, have, time, to, we, will)?

A: Yes, I think ²(hurry, if, up, we, will..., you).

B: Is it going to rain today?

A: No, the weather forecast says ³(be, definitely, fine, going, is, it, to), so you don't need your umbrella. Come on! Hurry up!

[B] Q&A

1. (　　　　) (　　　　) up earlier?
   (A) Peter.　　　　(B) Barbara.

2. Will they have (　　　　) (　　　　) to eat breakfast?
   (A) Definitely yes.　　(B) They might.

3. What is the (　　　　) (　　　　) to be like?
   (A) Fine.　　　　(B) Rainy.

Do you know?

Buckingham PalaceはSt. James's Parkの西端に⁽¹⁾あり、1837年のQueen Victoriaの即位⁽²⁾以来、王宮となっています。女王が滞在中は宮殿に王旗を掲げます⁽³⁾。毎日のように行われる衛兵交代式(The Changing of the Guard)は有名。夏のみ宮殿内部が公開されています。

(1) _____

(2) _____

(3) _____

Lesson 13   What Are You Doing?

進行形

イギリス人はサッカー好き

Warm Up!

37

1. How many people are there? (A) (B)
2. What is the woman holding in her right hand? (A) (B)
3. What is the man doing? (A) (B)

Check!

進行形

1. 進行中の動作・状態：be+ ...ing で、進行中の動作や状態を表す。

   Mr. Adams *is answering* the phone now. / I *was sleeping* when you called.

2. 不快・いらだち：alwaysを進行形と共に用いると、「〜ばっかり」という不快感を表す。

   John *is always* complaining. / Kathy *was always skipping* classes.

3. 一時的な行為や振るまいを表す。

   Margaret is usually nice and kind, but somehow she *isn't being* friendly today.

I Choose or Correct

1. Don't speak to the driver while he _____ .
   (A) is being driven (B) is driving
   (C) was being driven (D) was driving

2. We may be hit by a car while we _____ the street.
   (A) am crossing (B) are crossing
   (C) are being crossed (D) are crossed

3. I'll _____ you at the meeting held in the head office next week.
   (A) be being seen (B) be see (C) be seeing (D) be seen

4. I shouted at Robert, because he was _____ me.
   (A) always harassing (B) always harassed
   (C) hardly harassing (D) hardly harassed

5. Jane is usually quiet, but now, for some reason, she _____ .
   (A) be talkative (B) is been talkative
   (C) is being talkative (D) was talkative

6. <u>Are you knowing</u> why Chris <u>is absent</u>? He <u>is undergoing</u> an operation today.
       A   B   C

7. Diana <u>used to</u> <u>resemble</u> her father, but now she <u>is resembling</u> her mother.
            A   B   C

II Read and Answer

Steven is sitting at home reading a newspaper, and thinking about what to do tomorrow night. Barbie, his girlfriend, is having exams all week, so she is too busy to go out. The paper is full of stories about the big match. Liverpool is playing United tomorrow, and it is going to be quite a game. Steven's friend, Eddie, sometimes has spare tickets. "I wonder what Ed is doing right now, and I wonder if he is going to the match?" Steven is thinking.

Q & A

1. Why can't Barbie go to the match tomorrow?
   (A) She is away on holiday. (B) She is having exams every day.

2. Right now, Steven is ....
   (A) talking on the phone (B) thinking about tomorrow

III Write and Listen

[A] Arrange the words

(ring ... ring)

A: Hello, Steven? This is Barbie. What are you doing?

B: Hi Barbie. ¹(a, at, football, Eddie, game, I'm, with). Liverpool is playing Manchester United. It is freezing cold here, and it is raining. I am so cold I am shivering.

A: ²(is, like, match, the, what)?

B: There's no score yet... but just a minute.... Owen ³(ball, is, middle, running, the, the, up, with). He is going past one man, and now two. He's taking a shot, and it's a goal. And now Liverpool is leading one, nil. Barbie... are you listening?

[B] Q&A

1. Which two (　　　) (　　　) are playing each other?
   (A) Liverpool & Liverpool United.   (B) Manchester United & Liverpool.

2. What (　　　) (　　　) Steven shiver?
   (A) The cold weather.   (B) The exciting game.

3. What is Barbie (　　　) (　　　) this moment?
   (A) She is having dinner with Eddie.
   (B) She is talking on the phone to Steven.

Do you know?

ロンドンで、コンサートからギャラリー⁽¹⁾、レストランにいたるまで最新情報⁽²⁾を集めたい場合、情報週刊誌 "Time Out" か、街のいたる所で手に入るfree paper（無料のミニコミ誌）が便利です。情報を集めるだけでなく、現在のイギリスのエネルギー⁽³⁾が感じられ、文化的なおもしろい発見がたくさんあります。

(1) _____

(2) _____

(3) _____

Lesson 14

Using a Credit Card

完了時制

サイフを忘れたら支払いはカードで

Warm Up!

1. What is this man doing?　　　　　　　(A)　(B)
2. What is he wearing?　　　　　　　　　(A)　(B)
3. Can he use credit cards in this machine?　(A)　(B)

Check!

完了時制（過去完了、現在完了、未来完了）

1. 現在完了：現在までの完了・経験・継続を表す。
   I'*ve* just *finished* writing the paper. / We'*ve been married* for two years now.

2. 過去[未来]完了：過去[未来]のある時点までの完了・経験・継続を表す。
   I *had reached* the station before they arrived.
   I'*ll have finished* the report by noon.

3. 過去完了：過去のある時点より前の過去を表す場合がある。
   I was nervous when the plane left Narita, because I *had* never *been* abroad before.

I Choose or Correct

1. "Have you had any serious health problems?" "No, I've ____ healthy all my life."
   (A) be   (B) been   (C) being   (D) was

2. I can't remember his name, but I'm sure I ____ him somewhere.
   (A) don't meet   (B) didn't meet   (C) have met   (D) meets

3. By the time he retires, Mr. Brown ____ working for this company for 30 years.
   (A) is   (B) has been   (C) will be   (D) will have been

4. Just between you and me, everything ____ before the meeting began.
   (A) had been decided   (B) has been decided
   (C) will be decided   (D) would be decided

5. Bob said, "I ____ laid off for more than two years next week."
   (A) had   (B) has been   (C) will have   (D) will have been

6. Our president <u>has made</u> <u>an interesting</u> speech at <u>the conference</u> held yesterday.
                    A   B   C

7. "When <u>have you been to</u> Paris?" "I <u>went there</u> twice when I <u>was</u> a graduate student."
               A   B   C

II Read and Answer

It was Saturday and Robert had been shopping in Marks & Spencer's. He went to pay at the cashier's desk, but then he realized that he had left all his money at home. He decided to pay by credit card. "I've been living in this town for ten years, and I've been coming here every weekend, but it's the first time I have ever forgotten my wallet," he said.

Q & A

1. How long has he been living in this town?
   (A) For all his life.   (B) For ten years.

2. What was his new experience? It was the first time ....
   (A) he had forgotten his money
   (B) to go shopping in Marks and Spencer's

41

III Write and Listen 🎧 42

[A] Arrange the words

Robert: Last week something strange happened to me. When I
¹(finished, found, had, I, shopping, my) that I had no money with me.

friend: So what did you do?

Robert: I used my credit card.

friend: So ²(about, so, strange, that, what's)?

Robert: I've had a credit card since I left school, but I had never used it until that day. And do you know, it was ³(continue, easy, decided, I've, so, to, that) using it.

[B] Q&A

1. When did something (　　　) (　　　) to Robert?

    (A) When he left school.　　(B) When he finished shopping.

2. Why did Robert decide to (　　　) (　　　) card for the first time?

    (A) Because he had forgotten his wallet.　(B) Because it was so easy.

3. What has Robert decided to (　　　) (　　　) now?

    (A) Not to forget his wallet.　(B) To use his card more often.

Do you know?

イギリス人はあまり現金を持ち歩きません。かわりに、どんな少額⁽¹⁾でも小切手(cheque)を使う人が多いのに驚きます。小切手を使う場合は、銀行が一定金額までは支払いを保証する⁽²⁾cheque cardが必要です。旅行者はcredit cardを持っていれば、ホテルなどでは身分証明⁽³⁾のかわりにもなり便利です。

(1) ＿＿＿＿＿＿

(2) ＿＿＿＿＿＿

(3) ＿＿＿＿＿＿

Lesson 15 　　　　Museums

助動詞
ミュージアムはじっくり見よう

Warm Up! 　　　　　　　　　　　　　　　　　43

1. Wow! What is that?　　　　　　　　(A)　(B)
2. It looks like a ....　　　　　　　　　(A)　(B)
3. The sculpture is of a woman who is ....　(A)　(B)

Check!

助動詞

1. 一般的な助動詞：can, may, must, should, shall, will

   I'm not an actress yet, but I hope I *will* be in the future. / You *may* go now.

2. 2語以上から成るもの：be able to, have to, have got to, ought to,
   　　　　　　　　　　　be going to, used to

   You'll *have to* explain this data at the meeting. / I'll *be able to* drive a car next year.

3. 仮定法：助動詞の過去形 (could, would) は、仮定を表すことがある。

   I *could* call you (if you told me your number).
   A Japanese *wouldn't* do such a thing.

I Choose or Correct

1. _____ I take a day off tomorrow? I have a headache.
   (A) Can   (B) Do   (C) Will   (D) Would

2. There is a rumor that Judy is pregnant, but it _____ be true.
   (A) can't   (B) is not   (C) shall not   (D) will not

3. Emily once said, "I _____ have met Mr. Right."
   (A) can   (B) might   (C) ought   (D) ought not

4. I _____ not make a final decision. Let me ask our CEO about it.
   (A) can   (B) have to   (C) might have   (D) won't

5. Our company _____ probably invest in new equipment next month.
   (A) do   (B) must   (C) ought   (D) will

6. <u>Don't</u> forget to take your passport. You <u>will</u> <u>must</u> show it at the airport.
      A   B   C

7. "<u>This is</u> a small present <u>for you</u>." "Thank you. You <u>shall</u>."
      A   B   C

II Read and Answer   ♪ 44

That photo is of a sculpture by Henry Moore, and there are many more inside the museum. You don't have to pay any money to go in. However, you should leave your bags and cameras at the desk. We used to be able to take pictures of anything inside, but now we can't do that. Times have changed! The museum is quite big, so you should allow yourself about an hour to have a good look round. I think you will enjoy it.

Q & A

1. Do you need to buy a ticket for the museum?
   (A) Yes, you do.   (B) No, you don't.

2. What is it that you are not allowed to do any more?
   (A) Take photos.   (B) Leave your bags.

III Write and Listen

[A] Arrange the words

Tom: What did you think of that?

Steve: It was amazing. I hadn't realized that this museum had so many interesting things inside.

Tom: You 1(best, is, might, say, that, the, this) museum around here.

Steve: Yes, I think so. We should bring our wives and kids when we come again. I'm sure they would love it.

Tom: Oh, just look at the time! It's three. They 2(at, be, bus, ought, the, to, waiting) station. And we 3(an, been, half, have, hour, should, there) ago. Let's hurry.

[B] Q&A

1. Were Tom and Steve (   ) (   ) the exhibition?

    (A) Steve was. (B) They both were pleased.

2. Who are they going to (   ) (   ) their next visit to the museum?

    (A) Their colleagues. (B) Their families.

3. What (   ) (   ) Tom and Steve have been at the bus station?

    (A) At 2:30. (B) At 3:00.

Do you know?

ロンドンにあふれる美術館や博物館のなかでも、注目すべきなのは2000年にテムズ河畔に⁽¹⁾オープンした Tate Modern でしょう。Tate 美術館からモダン・アートのコレクション⁽²⁾を移し、主に20世紀以降の現代美術を展示しています。旧バンクサイド発電所⁽³⁾を改築した建物自体も一見の価値があり、ここからトラブルの末2002年にやっと開通した Millennium Bridge がかかっています。

(1) _____

(2) _____

(3) _____

Lesson 16　　　　　　The News

受動態
ちょっと表現が大げさなテレビニュース

Warm Up!

🎵 46

1. What is the woman looking at?　　　(A)　(B)
2. What is the woman wearing?　　　(A)　(B)
3. What transportation system is she going to use?　　　(A)　(B)

Check!

受動態

1. be 動詞+過去分詞：「～される」という動作や「～されている」という状態を表す。
   This shop *is closed* at 11 every night. ／ This shop *is closed* now.

2. get [become]+過去分詞：「～される」という動作を表す。
   I *got hurt* on my way home. ／ The truth *became known* as time went by.

3. 知覚動詞 (see, hear など)、使役動詞 (make など)：be動詞+過去分詞+to 不定詞の形
   Bill *was seen to* enter the room by everyone.
   Chris *was made to* work for nothing.

I Choose or Correct

1. Will you wait a moment? The report will ____ immediately.
   (A) be faxing   (B) be faxed   (C) fax   (D) get fax
2. I was frightened when I ____ by a stranger.
   (A) spoke to   (B) spoken to   (C) was spoken   (D) was spoken to
3. We should remind John that the deadline must ____ .
   (A) adhere to   (B) adhered to   (C) be adhered to   (D) be adhered to by
4. Albert ____ seriously injured in a traffic accident but recovered quickly.
   (A) became   (B) was   (C) grew   (D) were
5. Chris has just ____ to the CEO.
   (A) be promoted   (B) been promoted
   (C) being promoted   (D) was promoted
6. David was made go to buy some groceries by his mother.
            A   B   C
7. For further details, referred to the schedule that is enclosed herewith.
         A   B   C

II Read and Answer 47

Good evening and here is the news. A violent storm hit the small village of Meadowbank this morning. At least a dozen houses have been flooded near the river, and residents had to escape to high ground. Nobody was injured but trees were blown down, electric power lines were cut, roads were blocked and several cars were damaged. The local police say that repairs are being made, and that all services will be back to normal before the weekend.

Q & A

1. What happened to the village of Meadowbank this morning?
   (A) The village was hit by a storm.   (B) Several people were injured.
2. When will the residents be able to use the roads and electric power again?
   (A) In another month.   (B) Perhaps on Friday.

III Write and Listen

[A] Arrange the words

reporter: And ¹(happened, house, to, what, your)?

woman: It's a terrible mess. The downstairs rooms were flooded, and all the carpets and furniture have been ruined.

reporter: ²(about, how, rooms, the, upstairs)?

woman: Some roof tiles were blown off, and a lot of rain came in. My bedroom is completely soaked, but I ³(can, cleaned, get, it, think, we). I will have to have a lot of repairs done to the house and garden. And I will have to buy a new car, too.

[B] Q&A

1. (　　　) (　　　) to the carpets and furniture?

   (A) They were ruined.　　(B) They have become a little dirty.

2. Why did the upstairs rooms (　　　) (　　　)?

   (A) The house was old.　　(B) Some roof tiles had been blown off.

3. (　　　) (　　　) the woman going to do? She is going to....

   (A) buy a new car　　(B) repair the house by herself

Do you know?

イギリスのテレビは、国営のBBC (British Broadcasting Corporation)によるBBC1と2、民放⁽¹⁾の ITV(Independent TV)、Chanel 4と1997年に開局したChannel 5の5局しかないのですが、近年ではケーブルテレビ⁽²⁾も普及し始め、いろいろな番組⁽³⁾を楽しめるようになってきました。

(1) ＿＿＿＿＿＿

(2) ＿＿＿＿＿＿

(3) ＿＿＿＿＿＿

Lesson 17
to 不定詞

In the Park

休日は広々とした公園で

Warm Up!

1. How many girls are wearing sunglasses? (A) (B)
2. What are they doing here? (A) (B)
3. Who is the tallest? (A) (B)

Check!

To 不定詞

1. 名詞的用法：ask, decide, expect, promise, refuse, wish は to 不定詞のみ
   (cf. Lesson 18)

   To see is ***to believe***. ／ I decided ***to quit*** smoking.

2. 形容詞的用法

   I need someone ***to help*** me. ／ I'd like something ***to eat***.

3. 副詞的用法：目的（〜ため）、原因（〜して）、理由（〜だから）、結果（〜の結果）、
   条件（〜すれば）

   I'm sorry ***to have kept*** you waiting.
   To hear him talk, you'd think he was a professor.

I Choose or Correct

1. I'm sorry. I didn't mean ____ your feelings.
   (A) hurt   (B) hurting   (C) of hurting   (D) to hurt
2. If you want an autograph, you should bring something ____ .
   (A) to write with   (B) for writing   (C) with writing   (D) writing
3. Margaret applied for the position again, only ____ .
   (A) failed   (B) failing   (C) failure   (D) to fail
4. Julian left his hometown in his twenties, never ____ .
   (A) returned   (B) returning   (C) to return   (D) will return
5. Jane's father is said ____ something of a dandy in his youth.
   (A) being   (B) to be   (C) to have been   (D) having been
6. I can't stop <u>to smoke</u>, because <u>smoking</u> makes me <u>relax</u>.
             A   B   C
7. Don't forget <u>sending</u> a fax <u>to</u> Mr. Jones. He will be waiting <u>for</u> your reply.
                     A   B   C

II Read and Answer 50

Hello. We are on holiday in London. This morning we didn't know what to do, or where to go. It was my idea to come to this park and to hire these Rollerblades. At first it was difficult to stand up, but look at us now. Are you surprised to see how good we are? Well, we have to go now because I promised to meet a friend at the other end of the park. See you around! Bye!

Q & A

1. What did the girls want to do this morning?
   (A) They had no idea.   (B) They wanted to take a holiday in the country.
2. Why do they have to leave now? Because ....
   (A) they don't know what to do   (B) they have to meet a friend

III Write and Listen 🔊 51

[A] Arrange the words

Fiona: I couldn't do this at first, but now ¹(getting, hang, I'm, it, of, the).

Susan: Yes, me too. I really didn't want to go Rollerblading, but I'm beginning to enjoy it.

Fiona: What do you feel like doing now?

Susan: ²(about, bench, going, how, over, rest, that, to, to) for a few minutes? I'm getting tired.

Fiona: ³(anything, drink, like, to, would, you) ?

Susan: Thanks. Do you want to get me a Coke?

[B] Q&A

1. Has Susan started to change her (　　　) (　　　) Rollerblading?
   (A) Yes.　　　　　(B) Not really.

2. (　　　) (　　　) Susan suggest she would like to do?
   (A) To rest on the bench.　(B) To skate for a few minutes.

3. What is Susan's (　　　) (　　　) Fiona's offer?
   (A) I'll buy you a Coke.　(B) Could you buy a Coke for me?

Do you know?

公園はイギリス人の生活の一部です。ロンドンには大きな公園がたくさんあり、犬と一緒に散歩をしたり、木陰⁽¹⁾で読書やおしゃべりをしたり、ただ寝そべったり、サッカーをしたり、馬専用の道があって馬に乗っている人までいます。一年中⁽²⁾芝生は青々としているので、荒涼とした木々と緑の絨毯の美しいコントラスト⁽³⁾のなかを散策するのは、冬の楽しみのひとつです。

(1) ＿＿＿＿＿＿

(2) ＿＿＿＿＿＿

(3) ＿＿＿＿＿＿

Lesson 18　　　　　　　　　Walking

動名詞
散歩は暖かい格好で行こう

Warm Up! 🦆　　　　　　　　　　　　　　　🎧 52

1. Where is this gate?　　　　　　　　　　　　　　　(A)　(B)
2. The gate is locked, so how do hikers get to the other side?　(A)　(B)
3. The gate is always kept closed to ....　　　　　　　　(A)　(B)

Check!

動名詞（〜ing）

1. 名詞的用法：avoid, deny, enjoy, finish, imagine, mindは動名詞のみ
   (cf. Lesson 17)

   Smoking is not permitted here. ／ I enjoyed ***playing*** golf yesterday.

2. 形容詞的用法：「〜ための」という用途を表す。

   I'll be waiting for you in the ***dining*** car.

3. 慣用表現

   There is no accounting for tastes. ／ That book is ***worth reading***.

I Choose or Correct

1. Bob faced lots of difficulties to set up his business, but he never considered ____ .
   (A) give up   (B) giving up   (C) pick out   (D) picking out

2. Paul spent ten years ____ this project.
   (A) complete   (B) completing   (C) comply   (D) complying

3. The taxi driver was killed after ____ with the truck.
   (A) collide   (B) colliding   (C) correlate   (D) correlating

4. The essay Jeremy wrote is indeed childish in style, but its content is worth ____ .
   (A) look at   (B) of looking at (C) of reading (D) reading

5. The mayor was arrested yesterday on a charge of ____ a bribe.
   (A) take   (B) taking   (C) tame   (D) to tame

6. Despite <u>purchase</u> <u>many acres</u>, Brian didn't begin <u>to construct</u> a building.
         A   B   C

7. I know it's no use <u>crying over</u> <u>spilt milk</u>, but I can't <u>help complain</u>.
                        A   B   C

II Read and Answer 🔊 53

Walking is one of the most popular pastimes in this part of the country. At weekends many people enjoy hiking along paths like this one in the picture. Before leaving your house, you should think about taking enough food and warm clothes, and you should check the weather forecast. It's not worth getting caught in a storm when you are far from home.

Q & A

1. What do many people enjoy doing at the weekends in this part of the country?
   (A) They enjoy working.   (B) They enjoy walking.

2. Why should you check the weather forecast before leaving your home?
   (A) Getting caught in a storm is terrible.   (B) It is worth walking in a storm.

III Write and Listen 54

[A] Arrange the words

George: My idea of a perfect weekend is walking in the country and ¹(a, at, beautiful, day, looking, spending, scenery). What's yours?

Bill: Sitting at home, or watching TV, or even reading a good book is what I like best. I'm not keen on walking and I'm afraid of climbing, so staying indoors is perfect for me.

George: I prefer going out and travelling ²(house, in, needs, repairing, something, the, unless). It was a beautiful day last Sunday, but the grass needed cutting and the fence wanted painting.

Bill: I'm afraid I must be going now. ³(good, it, talking, was, with, you). See you again.

[B] Q&A

1. George is not (　　　　) (　　　　) on ....
   (A) watching TV　　　　(B) going out

2. Why did George have to (　　　　) (　　　　) home last Sunday?
   (A) He needed a haircut.　　(B) The grass was too long.

3. (　　　　) (　　　　) you describe Bill?
   (A) He is a couch potato.　　(B) He is an outdoor type.

Do you know?

イギリスではよく私有地⁽¹⁾に「侵入者は告訴されます」(Trespassers will be prosecuted.)という立て札⁽²⁾を見かけます。けれどもカントリーサイド⁽³⁾では、散策を楽しむ人々のために歩行者用の小道(public footpath)が確保されていて、にわか雨(shower)に備えてフード付きパーカ(parka)を着た人々が行き交います。

(1) ＿＿＿＿＿＿

(2) ＿＿＿＿＿＿

(3) ＿＿＿＿＿＿

Lesson 19   At a Hairdresser's

使役動詞

男でも髪を伸ばしたい

Warm Up! 　　　　　　　　　　　　　　　　　　　　　55

1. What kind of people get their hair cut here?　　(A)　(B)
2. In this hairdresser's you ....　　(A)　(B)
3. What is special about Saturday?　　(A)　(B)

Check!

使役動詞

1. 強制的使役make：make+人+原形動詞で、強制的使役「人に〜させる」を表す。
   Mike *made* his daughter *clean up* her room. ／ My mother *made* me *fix* a meal.

2. 許可の使役let：let+人+原形動詞で、許可の使役「人に〜させてあげる」を表す。
   If you buy a computer, *let* me *use* it. ／ *Let* me *go* now.

3. その他：have+人+原形動詞, get+人+to不定詞「人に〜させる、人に〜してもらう」
   I'll *have* him *fill out* this form.
   I usually *get* my husband *to* help me do the dishes.

I Choose or Correct

1. I wanted to go home to watch TV, but my boss ____ me work overtime.
   (A) got   (B) got to   (C) let   (D) made
2. ____ me stay up late tonight, because I have to prepare for the exam tomorrow.
   (A) Do   (B) Get   (C) Let   (D) Will
3. Do you think we should have our client ____ the bill?
   (A) pick up   (B) picking up   (C) picked up   (D) to pick up
4. I tried to get my son ____, but he said it would not be so worthwhile for him.
   (A) study abroad (B) studied abroad (C) studies abroad (D) to study abroad
5. If he won't apologize, I'll ____.
   (A) made him   (B) make him   (C) make him to   (D) make him to do
6. <u>Don't get</u> anyone enter <u>this room</u>, or else <u>I'll punish</u> you.
      A   B   C
7. Dad, can you <u>let me to use</u> your car? If you can't, <u>I'll</u> <u>get Jane to lend</u> me hers.
                                 A   B   C

II Read and Answer 56

Alan is sixteen and still at school. His mother lets him wear any kinds of clothes at the weekends, but his father is much stricter. He doesn't allow Alan to have long hair or earrings. Yesterday, he told Alan to get his hair cut. Alan wants to let his hair grow much longer, and he doesn't want his father to make him have it cut short.

Q & A

1. What doesn't his father allow Alan to have?
   (A) Earrings and long hair.   (B) Long hair.
2. What does Alan's mother let him do at the weekends?
   (A) Stay out late.   (B) Wear what he wants.

III Write and Listen

[A] Arrange the words

hairdresser: You can have your hair permed, or dyed. And I can cut it shorter, but I can't make it longer.

Alan: I want ¹(brown, have, it, on, to, top), and grey at the ends. I want to get a tight perm, and I want ²(a, like, look, make, me, rock star, to, you) from the 70s.

hairdresser: I can do that for you, but you might get a few strange looks from the people in the street. And your teacher might ³(down, have, hairstyle, to, toned, want, you, your) a bit.

Alan: I'm not worried about my teacher. It's my dad. He's going to hit the roof when he sees what I've had done.

[B] Q&A

1. What kind (   ) (   ) is Alan going to have?
   (A) Grey on top with brown stripes.   (B) Very curly with grey ends.

2. Who does Alan want to be made to (   ) (   )?
   (A) An old style rock star.   (B) His father.

3. How will Alan's father react when he sees his (   ) (   ) hairstyle?
   (A) He will become very angry.   (B) He will copy Alan's hairstyle.

Do you know?

最近、イギリス人のファッションにはアジア色が取り入れられています。漢字がプリントされたシャツやバッグ、タトゥー⁽¹⁾をよく見かけますし、回転寿司レストランも増え、幕の内弁当を目玉にした人気のレストランまであります。店内はたいてい、一見、和食屋⁽²⁾とは思えないシンプルな欧米風⁽³⁾で、ヨーロッパにうまく取り入れられた日本的要素を見ることができます。

(1) _____

(2) _____

(3) _____

Lesson 20　　　　　　　　Restaurants

someとany

レストランで注文を決めるのに、ひと苦労

Warm Up!　　　　　　　　　　　　　　　　　58

1. How many people can eat here for £5.50?　　(A)　(B)
2. Which meal is served with rice?　　(A)　(B)
3. What is the name of this restaurant?　　(A)　(B)

Check!

数量詞 some と any の用法

1. 肯定文にsome、疑問[条件]文にany

    I had *some* trouble with this computer. ／ Did you have *any* trouble?

2. 否定語+any = no〜(何も〜ない)：any+否定語という語順にならないことに注意

    I do*n't* have *any* money today. ／ Joan did*n't* have *anything* to do with this crime.

3. 肯定文で some (何か)、any (どんな〜でも)

    I'd like *something* to drink. ／ *Any* drink will do.

I Choose or Correct

1. I feel sick. Give me ____ medicine.
   (A) any   (B) any of the   (C) some   (D) some of the

2. Mr. Baker, there's ____ waiting for you at the door.
   (A) anyone   (B) everyone   (C) someone   (D) somewhere

3. Do you have ____ questions? If you do, ask me now.
   (A) any   (B) anywhere   (C) each   (D) something

4. If you have ____ difficulty using this copier, give me a call.
   (A) any   (B) little   (C) no   (D) some

5. Since I've got a lot of work to do, I'm very busy. I need ____ help.
   (A) any of the   (B) little   (C) some   (D) some of the

6. <u>Anything isn't</u> wrong with <u>this</u> computer. You don't <u>need to</u> call a repairman.
       A   B   C

7. I'm looking for <u>a hotel</u>. <u>Some hotel</u> will do as long as <u>it's</u> near the station.
             A   B   C

II Read and Answer

Look, two people can get some cheap meals in this restaurant. I might have some chicken pie with some chips and peas. Or maybe I'll go for a slice of pizza with chips. But there aren't any hamburgers on the menu, and there isn't any soup either. That's a pity. Er ... I can't make my mind up yet. Let's walk round the corner to the next place.

Q & A

1. Which is smaller, a slice of pizza or a pizza?
   (A) A slice of pizza.   (B) A pizza.

2. Where do you think they are going to eat?
   (A) Around the corner.   (B) They haven't decided yet.

III Write and Listen

[A] Arrange the words

waitress: ¹(order, like, to, you, would) now, sir?

man: Yes please. I want some mushroom soup, a steak, some chips and some fresh green peas.

waitress: ²(like, meal, some, tea, with, would, you, your)?

man: Yes, of course.

waitress: Do you want any cake or ice cream?

man: No, I don't want any cake, ³(but, ice cream, I, like, some, would), please.

[B] Q&A

1. What is the man going to (   ) (   ) his meal?

   (A) Some medicine.   (B) Some tea.

2. (   ) (   ) the waitress say "some" tea?

   (A) She thought the answer would be "yes".

   (B) She thought the answer would be "no".

3. What is the customer going to have (   ) (   ) ?

   (A) Some cake.   (B) Some ice cream.

Do you know?

今までイギリス料理というと roast beef や fish & chips のイメージ⁽¹⁾があるばかりだったのが、最近 modern British とよばれるレストランが増えています。伝統的なイギリス料理とエスニック料理⁽²⁾が融合した新しい味で、店内もシンプルながらファッショナブルな雰囲気⁽³⁾を醸し出しているところが多くなっています。

(1) _____

(2) _____

(3) _____

Lesson 21   Hotels

接続詞
古くても人気のあるホテル

Warm Up! 🎵 61

1. What is the name of the hotel in this photograph?   (A)   (B)
2. The hotel is attractive because it is ....   (A)   (B)
3. The hotel is a small ....   (A)   (B)

Check!

等位接続詞と従属接続詞

1. **等位接続詞**：and, but, or など文法上対等な関係にある語、句、文をつなぐ
   You *or* I have to be transferred abroad. / I had a headache, *but* I attended the class.

2. **従属接続詞**：as, because, if, when, since, thoughなど、主節と従属節をつなぐ
   Though Lynn is only 17, she is bilingual. / *If* you touch me, I'll call the police.

3. **特殊なもの**：suppose（もし〜なら）、provided, providing（〜という条件で）
   Suppose I got a million dollars, I'd buy a house. / I will go, *provided* you go too.

I Choose or Correct

1. I have a stomachache ____ I suffer from diarrhea.
   (A) and (B) but (C) however (D) or
2. Go to the dentist, ____ your decayed tooth will get worse and worse.
   (A) and (B) but (C) or (D) so
3. ____ I'm near-sighted, I rarely wear glasses.
   (A) Although (B) And (C) Because (D) When
4. I took a pill last night, ____ I had insomnia.
   (A) because (B) if (C) so (D) whether
5. ____ this medicine can cause a side effect, you should consult your doctor.
   (A) Although (B) Or (C) Though (D) Since
6. <u>But</u> Helen caught a cold, she recovered <u>from</u> it <u>without</u> seeing a doctor.
     A   B   C
7. <u>If</u> this surgery <u>will succeed</u>, Helen <u>will recover</u> completely.
    A   B   C

II Read and Answer 62

Since this hotel is in the centre of the city it is always full of tourists. It is so popular that unless you book early it is difficult to get a reservation. Although there is no convenient parking, most people arrive by car. Because the building is very old, the guests feel that they are living in a piece of British history. The rooms are small and the ceilings are low, but nobody ever complains.

Q & A

1. The hotel has a good location ....
   (A) so it is always full (B) because it is always full
2. Even though the rooms are uncomfortable ....
   (A) everyone is unhappy (B) the guests are pleased

III Write and Listen

[A] Arrange the words

guest: Hello. My name is Perkins, Trevor Perkins. I've reserved ¹(a, for, room, two, nights, with, you).

staff: Good evening, Mr. Perkins. We were expecting you earlier.

guest: Yes, ²(a, although, map, me, sent, you), I still couldn't find it. Look, since it has taken me such a long time to get here, I'd like dinner as soon as possible.

staff: Certainly sir. Would ³(eat, like, in, room, or, to, you, your) in the restaurant?

[B] Q&A

1. How long is Mr. Perkins going to (　　　) (　　　)?
   (A) Overnight.　　(B) For two nights.

2. ... he had a map, he (　　　) (　　　) the hotel.
   (A) Because　　(B) Even though

3. (　　　) (　　　) Mr. Perkin's request?
   (A) He wants to eat now.　　(B) He wants a map of the hotel.

Do you know?

イギリスの宿⁽¹⁾は、Youth Hostelから貴族の館（Manor House）をホテルにしたものまでさまざま。イギリスらしさが手軽に味わえるのは、B＆BとよばれるBed & Breakfast（朝食付き宿泊）で、特に田舎に行くと⁽²⁾、美しい庭の見える気持ちの良い部屋⁽³⁾と、ボリュームたっぷりのEnglish Breakfastが楽しめます。

(1) ＿＿＿＿＿＿

(2) ＿＿＿＿＿＿

(3) ＿＿＿＿＿＿

Lesson 22　　　　　　　　　Telephones

前置詞

故障が多い公衆電話

Warm Up!　　　　　　　　　　　　　64

1. How many people are there on the right of the telephone boxes?　(A)　(B)
2. Where is the litter bin? It is … the phone boxes.　(A)　(B)
3. There is a bench … the phone boxes.　(A)　(B)

Check!

前置詞：名詞、代名詞、動名詞 (…ing) の前に置く

1. 場所：at, in, above, on, over, among, between　など
   I'll stay *at* Namba *in* Osaka. / The airplane flew *over* the city.

2. 時間：at, on, in, for, since　など
   The meeting will start *at* 5 *on* Monday.
   My boyfriend was born *on* June 2 *in* 1971.

3. その他：by, of, from, to, through, with　など
   Paul is loved *by* everyone. / Judy is popular *with* young boys.

I Choose or Correct

1. Look at the schedule ____ the wall if you forget it.
   (A) above   (B) at   (C) in   (D) on

2. Go straight ____ this road, and you'll see the post office on your left.
   (A) among   (B) down   (C) in   (D) through

3. ____ a cold day in January 1995, a big earthquake took place.
   (A) At   (B) By   (C) In   (D) On

4. David is out for lunch. He'll be back ____ thirty minutes.
   (A) around   (B) during   (C) in   (D) into

5. The cover price of this magazine was 2 pounds, but I bought it ____ 1 pound.
   (A) by   (B) for   (C) in   (D) with

6. <u>Since</u> Ben has been working <u>in</u> Paris <u>during</u> 15 years, he speaks French fluently.
      A   B   C

7. Some of us are <u>for</u> the plan, but others are <u>against</u> it. So let's discuss it <u>on</u> lunch.
                     A   B   C

II Read and Answer 🎧 65

When you are in a hurry, public phones are always difficult to find. Last week, in the city centre, I had to walk for ages before I got to one. But that phone was out of order, and the next one was difficult to use. I had trouble with the instructions because I had forgotten my glasses. I am so disappointed with public phones that I'm thinking about getting a mobile.

Q & A

1. What was wrong with the first phone?
   (A) It was dirty.   (B) It wasn't working.

2. What is the elderly woman thinking about doing now?
   (A) Buying a mobile phone.   (B) Changing her glasses.

III Write and Listen

[A] Arrange the words

(ring... ring)

George: Hello, Brian? This is George. I've been ¹(but, can't, find, for, I, looking, you) you. Where are you?

Brian: Do you know Yates's restaurant? It's on the corner of High Street and Park Lane. I'm standing in a doorway, between the restaurant and the book shop on the right.

George: Oh no! I'm miles away at the bus station. Look, ²(don't, down, Park Lane, walk, why, you) towards the bus station and I'll walk up, and we should ³(about, bump, each, five, in, into, other) minutes?

Brian: Good idea. See you soon. Bye.

[B] Q&A

1. Where has George been (　　　) (　　　) Brian?
   (A) At the bus station.　　(B) Near the restaurant.

2. Where has Brian been (　　　) (　　　) George?
   (A) At the end of High Street.　(B) In a doorway.

3. Where are they going (　　　) (　　　) each other?
   (A) Somewhere along Park Lane.
   (B) On the corner of High Street and Park Lane.

Do you know?

イギリスのテレホンカードはphonecardと呼ばれるプリペイドカード⁽¹⁾で、カードの銀色の部分をこすると電話番号と暗証番号⁽²⁾が書かれてあり、そこに電話をかけてから相手先の番号を押すと、残り時間と料金が聞こえてきます。家庭用の電話機でも使え、種類も多く、カードによって値段も割引率⁽³⁾もさまざまです。

(1) _____

(2) _____

(3) _____

Lesson 23　　　　　　　　Haddon Hall

数詞

ダービーシャーにある古くて値打ちのある建物

Warm Up!　　　　　　　　　　　　　　　　　67

1. ... windows are open now.　　　　　　　(A)　(B)
2. What do you think this is a picture of?　(A)　(B)
3. Can you guess how old this building is?　(A)　(B)

Check!

数　詞

1. 基数詞(one, two, three)：dozen(12)が特殊。単数形の普通名詞とハイフンで接続
   Clovers usually have *three* leaves. / I found a *four-leaf* clover.

2. 序数詞(first, second, third)：通例theを伴う。
   The *first* son will be the heir. / I'm the *second* child.

3. 分数：分子から分母へ読む。「2分の1」は a[one] half、「4分の1」は a[one] quarter
   The bus will arrive at *a quarter to two*. (60分の4分の1は15分→2時15分前)

I Choose or Correct

1. George is only twenty-three years old, but he already has a ____ son.
   (A) one   (B) second   (C) two   (D) two old

2. We offer a ____ paid vacation to all the employees.
   (A) four-week   (B) fourth week   (C) fourth weeks   (D) week four

3. Would you go to the supermarket and buy two ____ ?
   (A) dozen of egg   (B) dozens of egg   (C) dozen eggs   (D) dozens eggs

4. At present, about one-third of the staff at the sales department ____ female.
   (A) are   (B) be   (C) is   (D) were

5. The company intention is to increase production ____ 25 percent over the next five years.
   (A) by   (B) manufacture   (C) since   (D) stock

6. Ben makes <u>two thousand pounds</u> <u>a year</u>, but his brother makes <u>third times as much</u>.
                 A   B   C

7. Since <u>this</u> is a quarterly magazine, we read it <u>four times</u> a year, that is, <u>every five months</u>.
        A   B   C

II Read and Answer 68

One of my favourite places in England is an old house in Derbyshire called Haddon Hall. The very first building here was recorded in the Domesday Survey in 1086. A quarter of the main house was built in the fourteenth century, and the remaining three quarters was added during the next 300 years. Today, it costs £5.90 to go in, which is about 1,125 in Japanese yen, and thousands of visitors come each year.

Q & A

1. How old is the oldest part of Haddon Hall?
   (A) About a hundred years old.   (B) More than 900 years old.

2. If two thousand people visit the house, how much money do they pay in total?
   (A) £8,850.   (B) £11,800.

III Write and Listen

[A] Arrange the words

A: Did you know that Haddon Hall was unoccupied for two hundred years from the 18th century? And after that ¹(all, buildings, restored, the, were).

B: Really? But did you know that in 1996 ²(a, couple, famous, here, made, movies, of, were)?

A: No I didn't. What were they?

B: One was Franco Zeffirelli's Jane Eyre, and the other was Elizabeth.

A: Wow! That's amazing!

B: Elizabeth I was the daughter of Henry VIII, and ³(from, queen, she, the, to, was, 1558, 1603).

[B] Q&A

1. (   ) (   ) was the house empty?
   (A) 20 years.　　　(B) 200 years.

2. (   ) (   ) the film called Jane Eyre?
   (A) Franco Zeffirelli.　　　(B) Henry VIII.

3. How long was Elizabeth the (   ) (   )?
   (A) For all her life.　　　(B) For forty-six years.

Do you know?

古いものを愛するのはイギリス人のひとつの精神です。100年ほどたった品々が無造作⁽¹⁾においてある家庭も多く、家は古いほど良しとされ、また地震がほとんどないこともあり、数百年前に⁽²⁾建てられた石造りの家⁽³⁾に今でも住んでいる人たちもいます。年月を経た古い館にはそこに住んできた人々の息遣いが感じられます。

(1) _____

(2) _____

(3) _____

Lesson 24　　　　Requests

丁寧表現
他人への依頼は丁寧に

Warm Up!

1. What colour is the woman's hair?　　　　(A)　(B)
2. What is the police officer wearing on his head?　(A)　(B)
3. What is the girl wearing on her left wrist?　　(A)　(B)

Check!

丁寧表現

1. 助動詞：Will[Can] you～?、Won't you～?、Would[Could] you～? などを使う。
   Would you take off your hat? / *Won't you* come and join us?

2. If you will[would] の使用：「もし～してくださるのだったら」という丁寧な依頼を表す。
   I'd be grateful *if you would* proofread my thesis. / I'll be glad *if you will come*.

3. 仮定法：仮定法過去で、丁寧な依頼や勧誘を表すことがある。
   Would it be all right *if I came* to your home before 5 o'clock?

I Choose or Correct

1. "Would you mind ____ I smoke?" "Not at all. Let me get you an ashtray."
   (A) as   (B) because   (C) if   (D) since

2. "Would you mind ____ the TV?" "Well, I'm watching it now."
   (A) I turning off   (B) my turning off   (C) turn off   (D) will turn off

3. I'm very thirsty. Would you mind ____ a cup of tea for me?
   (A) I making   (B) make   (C) making   (D) will make

4. If you ____ for one more week, I'll try to finish this term paper.
   (A) waited   (B) waiting   (C) waits   (D) will wait

5. It would be nice if you ____ overtime to finish this annual report.
   (A) work   (B) worked   (C) working   (D) works

6. "Would you getting that book on the shelf for me?" "I'm sorry, but I can't reach it."
      A   B   C

7. "Will you like a cup of coffee or tea?" "Thank you. I'd like a coffee, please."
       A   B   C

II Read and Answer 🔊 71

Mr. Brown is the general manager in an office. "Could you make me two copies of this report, please? And when you have done that I'd like another cup of coffee," he is saying to his secretary. Now he is talking to his boss. "I'm sorry to bother you, but would you mind if I go home half an hour early today, please? You see, it's my daughter's birthday and we are having a party for her."

Q & A

1. What did Mr. Brown ask his secretary to do?
   (A) Make some coffee.   (B) Make some copies and some coffee.

2. Why was Mr. Brown's last request such a long one? Because ....
   (A) he was talking to his boss   (B) he was happy

III Write and Listen 🎧 72

[A] Arrange the words

Peter: Hello Dad, how are you?

Mr. Jones: Oh hello, Peter. I'm ¹(better, much, than, yesterday), thank you.

Peter: Do you want me to do anything for you?

Mr. Jones: Could ²(for, me, on, the TV, turn, you), and get me a glass of water, please? Oh, and ³(closing, mind, the, window, would, you)? It's getting a bit cold in here.

Peter: Would you like anything else, Dad?

Mr. Jones: No thanks. That's all.

[B] Q&A

1. (   ) (   ) Peter want to do?

    (A) To help his father.   (B) To drink some water.

2. Did Mr. Jones "ask" or "tell" Peter to (   ) (   ) things?

    (A) He asked Peter.   (B) He told Peter.

3. Why did Mr. Jones want Peter (   ) (   ) the window?

    (A) The sunshine was too strong.   (B) The room was becoming cold.

Do you know?

イギリスの風土や生活、家庭について楽しみながら知るひとつの方法は、子どもの本を読んでみることです。日本でもおなじみの⁽¹⁾『不思議の国のアリス』や『クマのプーさん』、『ピーターパン』や『ピーターラビット』、『メアリー・ポピンズ』も、そしてベストセラーの⁽²⁾『ハリー・ポッター』も全部イギリスのお話です。原書を読んで⁽³⁾みませんか？

(1) _____

(2) _____

(3) _____

Lesson 25

付加疑問

Going Home

帰るときは、みやげものでいっぱい

Warm Up! 🎵 73

1. In which direction are these people walking?　(A)　(B)
2. What kind of day is it?　(A)　(B)
3. What can you say about the hotel?　(A)　(B)

Check!

付加疑問文

1. 通常の付加疑問文：肯定文＋否定、否定文＋肯定

   You got a pay raise, *didn't you*? / *You didn't* attend the class, *did you*?

2. 命令文の付加疑問文：命令文＋will[would] you?

   Turn off the light, *will you*? / Go home before dark, *would you*?

3. Let's の付加疑問文：Let's..., shall we?

   Let's go get a drink, *shall we*? / *Let's* play baseball, *shall we*?

I Choose or Correct

1. You told me yesterday you were from Ireland, ____ ?
   (A) are you   (B) can you   (C) didn't you   (D) don't you

2. Always be polite no matter how well-qualified you are, ____ ?
   (A) are you   (B) aren't you   (C) do you   (D) would you

3. Our section chief proposed the plan, ____ ?
   (A) does he   (B) doesn't he   (C) didn't he   (D) wasn't it

4. Let the small children enter the room before you, ____ ?
   (A) shall I   (B) shall you   (C) will you   (D) will we

5. Let's take a break before we go on to the next item on the agenda, ____ ?
   (A) shall I   (B) shall we   (C) will you   (D) won't you

6. Last week you and I made a decision on this matter together, didn't you?
            A   B   C

7. You didn't have enough money to set up a branch office, don't I?
         A   B   C

II Read and Answer 🎧 74

Bring your suitcases and bags over here, will you? Now, Pamela, you've two bags and a suitcase, haven't you, and Karen's got three and a case, hasn't she? I'll just put them together in this corner. Right, that's three suitcases and six bags including mine, isn't it? Pam, your case weighs a ton, doesn't it? What have you got inside it? You've bought half of England, haven't you?

Q & A

1. How much luggage did the man bring?

   (A) One suitcase and one bag.   (B) Three suitcases and a bag.

2. Why does the man think Pamela's suitcase is so heavy?

   (A) She did too much shopping.   (B) She has a one ton weight inside it.